MW01297116

A compelling story of coming-of-age with autism.

Los Angeles Times, December 2011

An emotional and inspiring book that will benefit anyone with autism and their families.

Reno Gazette Journal, February 2012

INSIDE OUT

2013 Literary Excellence Recipient, International Naturally Autistic People Awards, Vancouver, Canada

2012 Honorary Mention, New York Book Festival

i

INSIDE OUT

Stories and Poems from an Autistic Mind

RUSSELL LEHMANN

Library of Congress Control Number: 2011918257
ISBN: Hardcover   978-1-4653-7883-5
               Softcover   978-1-4653-7882-8
               Ebook   978-1-4653-7884-2

To order additional copies of this book, or to book Russell for an event, please visit:

www.TheAutisticPoet.com

or

www.Russell-Lehmann.com

CONTENTS

INSIDE OUT

ACKNOWLEDGEMENTS

I would like to thank my parents, for without them I would not be where I am today, and my sister, who has always offered her ears whenever I am having a tough time. I also have to thank my high school football coach, Jason Ehlen. He has been a blessing and has helped me through all of the problems that arose during my high school years.

WORD FROM THE AUTHOR

I wrote this book back in 2011, and all the statistics and facts presented in this book are from that year. During the time I wrote this book, I was still trying to find my true calling in life. Did I want to be a poet? A journalist? A professional athlete? A rapper? All of these careers had one thing in common: I wanted to use my experiences as an individual on the spectrum, and the lessons I've learned from them, to help others.

In May of 2015, I finally decided with the utmost certainty what career path was best suited for me, and I haven't looked back since. I am now a motivational speaker who travels the country spreading hope, awareness, acceptance and understanding about autism, while encouraging others to embrace their challenges, for they make us who we are.

I could not let all the pain and agony I've been through, and still continue to go through, to be for nothing. I needed to share my story and advice in order to be a voice for the unheard, for I know how frustrating and challenging it is to go unnoticed. I'm honored and humbled to be able to give hope to families and parents who are concerned with their child's future, just as my parents once were. I let kids who are struggling with *anything*, know that no matter how cliché it sounds, life DOES get better, you just have to believe it will.

For more information about me and my journey, I encourage you to visit my website www.TheAutisticPoet.com. I am currently in the midst of writing my second book, but in the meantime, I hope you enjoy this one.

My Very Best,
Russell

INSIDE OUT

INTRODUCTION

Inside Out: Closed on the outside, open on the inside. That's how I would describe myself living with autism. Throughout my whole life I have walked the long, lonely roads and have struggled to come out of many valleys. I have also had some triumphs, and poetry is one of them. I have written many poems that range from the mental and emotional struggles that are destined in life, my own personal hardships, as well as Mother Nature, Darfur, and much more. There are two very different styles of writing in this book. First, in the timeline of events that have taken place in my life, the writing may seem somewhat flat. Since I have autism, it is very hard for me to communicate with others on a daily basis. This is reflected throughout my autobiography. It is difficult to talk, and therefore write about my life in an expressive manner. However, I believe my poems make up for that. Many of them are very deep and thought-provoking. When I am trying to communicate with someone, all of these complex thoughts fill my head and I can't figure out what to say. The easiest way for me to express these thoughts is through poetry. My hope is that the contrast between the writings in this book will help to give you a sense of what it is like living with autism.

Having autism is hard. However, having high-functioning autism can sometimes be even harder. For example, when a high-functioning autistic person communicates with a stranger, oftentimes the stranger doesn't realize the person has a disability; therefore, you are looked upon as odd, scared, and sometimes even stupid. My name is Russell Lehmann. I am twenty-one years old, and I have high-functioning autism.

The autism rate today is 1 in 110. However, back in 1990, the year I was born, autism was very rare. Throughout the United States, 1 out of every 10,000 children was diagnosed with autism. In California, for kids who were five years-old and younger, the autism rate was even lower, at 0.8 per 10,000 children. Finally, in Denmark, the autism rate for kids who were two to four years old was a staggering 0.5 per 10,000 children.

I have been living with OCD (obsessive-compulsive disorder) my whole life and did not find out that it was abnormal until the age of nine. My OCD affected me every second of every day. Only when I fell asleep was I released from the horrible disorder. Every single thing that I looked at would have to be looked at an even number of times, specifically in multiples of four (4, 8, 16, 32, 64, sometimes all the way up to 256). If I did not complete this task or if I looked at something an odd number of times, I would be bombarded by horrible thoughts, such as loved ones dying in gruesome scenes, me killing my family members, our house catching on fire. The list goes on and on.

Since the age of eight, I have been taking a cocktail of medications. The first medicine I had to take was Concerta. My doctor back then had no clue as to where my symptoms were stemming from, so he just slapped the label of ADHD on me and called it a day. As I became older, I started taking more and more medications. None of them seemed to work. Finally, after many years of experimenting, I was taking a mix of five medications that seemed to be doing their job. I still had extreme anxiety, OCD, and depression, but a little relief went a long way.

All the medications I have ever taken have had major side effects on me. Lifting weights and being extremely active have always been my greatest coping method. However, medications have always inhibited my ability to do that. One of the worst occasions was when I tried out

for high school basketball in 2006. When the coach made us sprint non-stop up and down the court, I began to lose my sight very quickly. I became extremely dizzy and felt all the blood rushing to my head. I obviously had to stop sprinting. When the coaches saw me stop, however, they yelled at me and told me to act like I wanted to be there. I have always been an extremely hard worker and basketball was my life, so those comments really hurt. I started sprinting again even though my eyesight was 50 percent.

I was able to make it to the end of the drill, and when I did, my muscles were so exhausted that I fell to the floor. I had the worst headache, and for a minute or so, I could see nothing but black.

In 2010, I started working with a personal trainer so that I could play college football. The very first time I met with him, however, I lost both my sight and ability to hear. This was very unusual because I was only working out very lightly as opposed to the extreme regimen that I go through. I freaked out, and I had to be taken to the emergency room. They ran multiple tests and said that my blood pressure was unusually low. I was released after about six hours in the ER and was instructed to take it easy for a good week.

To this day, I still have many side effects from my medicine. When I am playing pickup basketball, my throat closes up to the point where I can barely breathe. When I exercise, my saliva thickens and becomes stuck in my throat due to my medication. I very frequently get dizzy to the point where I have to sit down, and when I move my eyes, I can hear a buzzing sound every time they change direction to look somewhere. The best way for me to describe it is the sound of a sword being pulled from its sheath.

I have always been extremely frustrated that my ability to perform my best when it comes to sports is hindered by my medications. I know that all these symptoms are not at all good for my health, but sports are my life and I literally could not live without it. I have also debated, many times, whether I should go off my medications, but whenever I tried to wean off one, my anxiety, OCD, and depression would increase tenfold.

1990–1995

I was born December 5, 1990. My parents were extremely excited because they had had three miscarriages before me. However, the day turned out to be pretty terrifying for them. Right when I was born, my entire body was dark blue due to lack of oxygen. I was also (in the doctor's words) very floppy, meaning that I had poor muscle tone for a baby. He said that this was also due to lack of oxygen. Luckily, once he gave me oxygen, I responded right away. The blue drained from my body, and my skin color started to become normal. During the first couple of months in my life, I slept much more than the average baby. I also did not move my arms very much and had slightly delayed motor skills. I did not learn to sit up until I was nine months old, the average being five months. The doctors thought nothing of it and said it was just because I was a big baby (I was born 9 lb. 3 oz.). By the time I was two years old, I was still not talking at all. If I wanted something, I would just point and grunt. Finally, after three long years, I started to make progress with my speech.

When I was three, I started blacking out quite often. The very first time was when my grandpa was visiting. My mom and he were talking at the kitchen table, and I was right outside sitting on a bench eating a yogurt. All of a sudden, my mom saw all the color drain from my body and I immediately slouched over, totally out cold.

My mom rushed out and put her hands on my shoulder. It took a good amount of time, but I eventually came around. I got up right away, and for the rest of the day, I acted perfectly normal. The next time was when my uncle came to visit. I opened the front door as he arrived and ran outside. Not twenty seconds later, I dropped to the ground, once again losing all consciousness. My mom, dad, and uncle ran over to me and saw that I was dark blue. It didn't take long for me to wake up this time, but when I did, I started crying. Later that week, my mom and I were standing in our driveway when, once again, she saw all the color drain from my body. She knew what to expect this time, so she was able to catch me as I dropped to the ground.

This time, I did not lose consciousness, but I was very dazed and confused. My parents immediately called the doctor on call (it was the weekend), and he met us at the hospital. He scheduled numerous tests to be done later that week, including an EEG (electroencephalography). When my parents finally received the results, nothing abnormal showed up. They didn't know whether to be scared or happy. Throughout the next ten months, I kept having these episodes. My parents were able to learn the signs when I was about to collapse. I would completely freeze and stop breathing. They would tell me, in a loud voice, to breathe and would gently shake me. At once, I started to breathe again and acted as if nothing had happened.

Throughout the ages of six to ten, my mother was a respiratory therapist who worked the night shift at Children's Hospital in Seattle. Below is a written account of this experience that I recently wrote for a class in college.

Through the Storm Comes Love

The last day of the weekend never did treat me well. It was an early winter night and the darkness started to prevail. A storm was brewing, not just in the sky, but in my mind. It was 7 o'clock, and my mother was getting ready to leave for work. As a respiratory therapist, her job was to help save people's lives. My life however, felt far from saved once she walked out the front door. I was a young boy, not yet ten, who suffered from severe separation anxiety. Every Sunday night, my mother was scheduled to work the night shift at Children's Hospital in Seattle, and one week never went by without me pleading for her to stay home. The pain was immense. Twin rivers would flow down my cheeks, and, merging at my chin, would empty into my heart, the ocean of my pain. How could this winter night become ever darker?

The time had finally come for my mother to leave. She gave me a kiss, bent down, and told me not to worry. As she hesitantly closed the door (for I am sure she did so with much pain), one could say that I embodied a tornado. Flying up the stairs, the salty rain began to pour. I would rush into my bedroom closet and slam the door; the thunder had begun. My father (you could call him a storm-chaser, I suppose) remained calm and waited for the rain to stop. Once this fulfillment was obliged, he opened the doors to my closet. I knew what he was going to say, yet in some obscure fashion, I did not know what I was going to hear. "Think you're ready to go get some ice cream now?" At last, the storm was beginning to pass.

As my father drove us down to our local ice cream shop, the skies had started to clear. The shimmer of the moon gleamed down upon the building with such grace, almost as if it was guiding us toward happiness or, should I say refuge, if perhaps the storm were to come back. Once inside, I felt like a kid in a candy store, only this time it wasn't candy, but ice cream. It took me not five seconds to decide what I was going to get. Without hesitation, I told my father that I wanted the vanilla ice cream with chunks of Reese's peanut butter cups. However I didn't need to tell him that, for he already knew that it was the main part of my recovery effort.

This storm continued to persist every Sunday for many years, throughout which the same outline of events routinely unfolded. How was it that the foundation on which I was built continued to stand?

This wasn't a matter of luck, or even persistence on the part of me, but a feeling of unity so tightly bound through love of what one may call a family. Of course, I only gained this insight a few years after the storm had, at long last, finally cleared. To think back and look upon this whole experience from a much matured outlook, I wonder what lessons I may have learned.

For one, I know now that love and acceptance from a family cannot be expected. A force of nature, such as a storm, puts to the test not only the strength of those affected, but of those who surround the affected. For as I said, love and acceptance does not come from those who are in the eye of the storm, but from those whose life and well-being depend on the resources that each of us is born with. However, you mustn't take my word for it, for you should soon discover it yourself.

Through hardships comes perseverance, through adversity comes strength, and through storms comes love. This, my friends, is surely the greatest gift of all.

2000

In March, I came down with a severe case of bronchitis. I was not able to attend school for two weeks. I became so comfortable in my own house that when I had recovered, I didn't want to go back to school. There was so much anxiety building up inside me that I eventually became agoraphobic. My mom would always try to help me muster up the courage to walk down to the bus stop, but I could never do it. There were some occasions that I was able to start walking to the bus stop, but once I started to draw closer and saw all my friends, I made a beeline for home.

After a good week of repeating this, my mom thought of a different approach. She'd have me get ready for school in the morning, and then she would drive me down to school in our car. I was very excited and optimistic about this plan. Even though I was scared to go near them, I missed my friends with all my heart. I would wake up in the morning feeling good and confident that I could overcome this endeavor. However, when the time came to get in the car to leave, my mind went into overdrive. I was hit with major panic attacks and would drop to the floor and curl up in a ball. My mom, who suffered from anxiety herself, and per the advice of my doctor, thought that if I worked through this and was able to take that step into the classroom, I would start to calm down and begin to go with the flow. This would have been the right thing to do if your child *only* suffered from anxiety. Little did we know that this was not the case with me. When I was finally able to stand up and walk to our garage door, I would freeze underneath the doorframe. My sole objective was to not take a single step outside of my house. My mom, being extremely stressed out and not knowing what to do, along with the fact that I couldn't miss another day of school, grabbed me around the waist and tried to usher me into the car. With all my might, I grabbed hold of the doorframe and hung on for my life. Sobbing and screaming at the top of my lungs, my mom, who was crying herself, pulled and pulled, but I would just not let go. She finally gave up, knowing that all she was doing was making it worse. I was allowed to go back into the house, and I ran straight up to my room and hid in my bed. This scene repeated itself for the next week, with me gradually making as much progress as to be driven down to the school. But once again, when it was time for me to get out of the car, I shut down into panic mode.

My mom tried to comfort me and told me that she would walk to my class with me, but it was no use. Once again, per the instructions of my doctor, she tried pulling me out of the car. And once again, I hung on to the car door, refusing to let go. Of course, I was also sobbing and screaming again. But my mom knew better. She never wanted to make me feel worse, and I can't even imagine how she felt trying to force me out of the car. She discarded the doctor's advice, knowing that what she was doing was making the situation extraordinarily worse. She drove me home and called the school for the twentieth time in as many school days to let them know that I was not going to be able to make it in.

I ended up staying home for three and a half months. My mom would pick up schoolwork for me to do at home, but I was in such a bad shape that I was not able to function mentally.

The day that I was finally able to go back to school was excruciatingly terrifying. My biggest phobia was being bombarded with all my friends' questions as to why I stopped going to school. I was one of the most popular kids, so I knew that every single kid was going to ask me something. All I could say to them was "I don't know" or "Because." At this point in my life, I started wearing a hoodie over my head whenever I went out in public, especially when I went to school.

In April, I had a severe allergic reaction to one of my medications. I was very happy that evening because we were eating my favorite meal—macaroni and cheese. During dinner, however, my throat began to swell shut. I couldn't eat, and it was extremely hard for me to breathe. This theme seems to constantly occur in my life. Once something good is going for me or when I am just simply happy, everything starts to turn for the worse. This was one of those times.

That night was definitely one of the scariest moments in my life. I was crying so much and kept asking my mom if I was going to die. I can't imagine how that made her feel, a mother's own child scared he was going to die. This is one of the worst things about having autism that many people do not know. It kills me inside to be going through such pain while also knowing that you are possibly destroying your own family's lives.

My parents had to call 911, and an ambulance was rushed over to our house. I can still remember our neighbors looking through their window as I was lifted into the ambulance. I wondered why I couldn't be on the other side of that window. I ended up spending four hours in the ER. The doctors gave me a breathing treatment with epinephrine, and my throat finally started to open up. My family and I were all extremely relieved. I never thought that breathing could be so enjoyable.

About two days later, my family and I went on a vacation to Europe. This two-week trip would turn out to be pure hell. We had had this trip planned for a good year. Even though I was experiencing extreme anxiety lately, we stood to lose thousands of dollars if we canceled the trip. Plus, I kept telling everybody that I would be just fine.

The very first day we were there, I started to feel uncomfortable. We had landed in Charles de Gaulle Airport in Paris, France, and I could already tell how different their culture was. I'm sure some of it was just my imagination, but people looked and dressed totally different, which scared me. Throughout this two-week trip, we also visited Switzerland and Germany. There were a lot of fun times; however, the rest of the time I was totally out of control due to being extremely anxious and overwhelmed.

Our whole family was torn apart during this vacation. We were constantly at one another's throats and everyone was very upset with me because they didn't fully understand what I was going through. I refused to eat *anything*, not even American food like McDonald's or simple sandwiches. I ended up having several severe panic attacks and extreme bouts of depression. My OCD was also through the roof. I cannot even try to explain the mental anguish that I was going through. I was only nine years old and had already lived through a lifetime of problems.

2001

In May of 2001, when I was in fourth grade, summer was approaching very fast. Up until this time, I had had a great overall school year. However, I started to get very overwhelmed with all the commotion that comes at the end of the school year. My class was planning a field trip to the zoo, and I was very excited about this. But sometimes, my excitement gets the best of me.

One morning before school, out of the blue, I was terrified to leave the house. I was very worried that this would turn into the same debacle that happened during the previous school year. I stayed home that day, hoping that I would feel better the following day.

Unfortunately, my anxiety would not stop growing. I really missed my friends and did not want to lose contact with them once again. I also dreaded the possibility of missing out on the field trip. All in all, I ended up missing two weeks of school. I was finally able to muster up the courage of going back to school, but not before the field trip had come and gone. I finished the last week of the school year and really believed that I had finally conquered my demons. Soon, though, they would come back to conquer me.

2002

One morning in May of 2002, I had an appointment with my orthodontist to have my braces removed and to be given a retainer to use. After the appointment, my mom drove me to school. It was around 10:30, and I was scheduled to go into one of my favorite classes: music. I knew that the music teacher was going to let us watch a movie and give us popsicles. I was really looking forward to it until I was driven up to the front of the school. Once again, however, I started to have an extreme panic attack and could not get out of the car. After about ten minutes, my mom finally coaxed me out. I was able to take a few steps toward the front doors, but then froze. I couldn't walk any farther. Crying, I told my mom that I couldn't do it. She asked me if I was sure, but I know that she already knew the answer. I climbed back into the car and was finally taken home. My heart sank to my stomach. I knew that I was letting myself down, but I also felt that I was letting my mom down. I couldn't help but think that she thought I just didn't like school and that I was taking the easy way out even though I knew that she didn't.

As I looked back at the school, I knew that I had just started the same game that I had played in third and fourth grade. However, this time I had the feeling that that I was not going to win. This was the last day I would ever participate in public school again. This was the day that ended all my relationships with my friends and, ultimately, led to the complete destruction of my childhood. However, the symptoms of autism started to destroy my life when I was eleven. The most problematic symptoms in my life are OCD, anxiety, and depression.

2003

Cursed to Be Normal

I was cursed to be normal, the normality of strange
God must have been drunk when he put together my brain
I feel like I've been stuck at level 1 of this game
This game of tolerating pain, which I have done without gain
Problems with me are too much to feel ashamed
Of what has been going on inside of my brain
Since day 1×30 days multiplied by 72 ways
I have proclaimed I need help, to change my way of self-esteem
For it has been high every day
Even though it seems there are no means,
To confiscate the compliments I put away in my dreams
This part of me seems so ugly in the way
That it seems to deem my inner retard every day
I'm sorry if that offends you in some close-minded way
But just think this thing inside of me comes out every day
Much to my dismay
I feel like I should fly away up to the heavens
And ask God
Why me?

INSIDE OUT

I was 12 when I said I was 13
I wanted to fit in and not lose myself

Over this OCD
So I sat in C-3 for five straight strenuous weeks
Until the doctor came and told me
That my treatment was complete
I was free

I was happy at first, but later on that day
I grew angry because the doctor didn't tell me
That there was another school I had to see

Simple minds and simple times occurred inside that school
Except for me, for I had my hood up
And drifted off to some tunes
When I was forced into a room of complete solitude
All the while knowing that those people had played me for a fool
All they ever did was look for somebody to screw

Mrs. Yappity-Yap and Mr. Do-This-and-Do-That
Were so irritating! They thought they had me in their laps
But I just blew them off and took three-hour naps
Until my mom picked me up and drove me away from that trap
I would look back and pray that I wouldn't have to go back

These ideas stem from a mind
That has been through too much in its time
So calloused it has become in its long worn-out life
From attempts to colonize the insults it has survived
And throw them off to the side

I wish I could give them my life and see the fear in their eyes
As they cry and apologize for the damage they have done
To a life so young
And now that life is saying "So long,
You are in the past
For my life has just begun."

Since day 1 I've been in crisis mode
I cannot even begin to relate
To what a normal life feels like
Until I look it in the face

But still then
I don't see any eyes, ears, nose, or mouth
I just see a black hole
That is the epitome
Of what my life is about
But I just keep on staring in the mirror
Trying to figure my life out

My OCD is bittersweet
In the fact that it hurts me and my family
In the fact that it forces me to always perform superbly
In the fact that when I go to sleep, I count sheep infinitely
In the fact that I cannot stop until I succeed in everything
Until I'm close to fainting
I train hard because training
Puts a positive reinforcement in me
That I can be anything that I want to be
Say hello to this positive reinforcement, please
His name is OCD
And right now, he is the manipulator that I want him to be
But then there's a flip side, for he can always turn real mean
He becomes so very angry that he thinks the thoughts in me
And spits out the nasty spews of his tongue indefinitely
And unfortunately, his tongue is the one I use to speak
So please, somebody help me
For this OCD
Has become the being of existence
That is supposed to be me.

In 2003, my anxiety, OCD, and depression became so bad that I was admitted to Children's Hospital. I was somewhat excited because, in my mind, I was picturing a very relaxing room where my family and

I could all be together and talk things out. However, once I got there and was taken to the psychiatric unit, I saw that it was extremely chaotic and noisy. The doctors took my parents and me into a conference room for admittance. They asked my parents some questions about my background and what their hopes were for admitting me there. After about twenty-five minutes, one of the counselors came in to show me to my room. I refused to go and started to break down. I didn't think there was any way I could survive in there without either one of my parents. The doctors promised me that I would only be away from my parents for just a couple of minutes. I trusted them because I knew that if I didn't, I would not make any progress toward my recovery. I grudgingly went with the counselor, who introduced me to my roommate. I was definitely in no mood to talk.

Once I got to my room, I stood as still as a statue. Looking out the second-story window and crying, I comforted myself by thinking that my parents would be there any minute. I waited and waited and waited. I never took my eyes off the window, all the while crying. As the time went by, I grew angrier and angrier. It had been like what seemed forever, and the doctors never even bothered to send someone to give me an update. In the end, I looked out that window, crying my eyes out while never moving once, for a good two hours before my parents finally arrived.

I ended up staying there for five weeks. Those weeks were, by far, the worst my family and I had ever experienced. There were certain nights when my parents would be able to take me out for an hour or two. One night, my dad came to take me to a movie. Before we left, he gave me three basketball posters for me to put up in my room. I was so excited! I can still remember unrolling them and being in somewhat of a trance. I had been through so much lately that a simple gift like this really cheered me up.

When we arrived at the movie theater, I started to become very anxious. It was a very small privately owned theater and, for me anyway, in a gloomy part of Seattle. As we walked inside, I started to have a panic attack. I was able to hold myself together as we went and got popcorn and made the walk upstairs into the lone theater. As we sat down, I didn't become more anxious; I became more scared. I was extremely afraid of all the people around us, and being in the dark didn't help either. I told my dad that I couldn't stay there. He was hesitant to get up and asked me if I was sure. I was already crying from having a panic attack, but the guilt I felt was tremendous. Once again, I felt that I was letting my dad down. That evening was supposed to be nothing but fun, a brief escape from the prison that I was in.

We left the theater and walked back to our car. I could tell that my dad was in so much pain from seeing me like this. As we got into the car, he started to break down and cry. I felt like I wanted to die. As we drove away from the theater and back to the hospital, I knew that something bad was going to happen.

We were driving down a hill, and at the bottom, there were cars stopped at a red light. Farther and farther down the hill we went, both of us sobbing in pain. I could see that we weren't slowing down, and we crashed right into the back of the car in front of us. My popcorn flying everywhere, none of us were affected from the crash. We were already way beyond any disturbance a crash could give us. My dad got out of the car and started to exchange information with the two women whose car we hit. I remember one of the women coming up to me and asking if I was okay. I just nodded as tears dripped into the remains of the popcorn that I started to devour.

I was supposed to be back at the hospital at seven, but I wasn't able to get there until eight thirty. Everything that had happened was starting to sink in, and though somewhat in shock, I walked straight into my room. That night was, by far, the worst night in my life. I can't even put into words the mental destruction that had occurred to me that night. I also will never be able know what was going through my dad's head that night. To this day, I feel so at fault of what had transpired that torturous night. I was in so much emotional pain that it tore us apart. I still cannot believe that we were able to stick it out and prevail.

While in the hospital, the main therapy that the doctors subjected me to was to confront my fears. I was extremely afraid of bugs, so every day they had me pick up dead bumblebees. Obviously, I was also scared to death of going to public school, so they had me attend a class here and there. I also had major separation anxiety from my mom, so they would not allow her to see me for extended amounts of time.

As I look back on these events, I still can't understand what those doctors were thinking. However, I don't regret what had happened. I believe that it played a huge part into making me who I am today.

Throughout those five weeks, the only symptom that had improved was my OCD. My anxiety and depression were still sky-high, and the doctors had no clue as to what diagnosis to give me. In the end, the doctors gave up and discharged me. This was one of the happiest days of my life. It was the first time that I had ever cried out of happiness. Little did I know, though, that the doctors had enrolled me in my public middle school, which I was to attend immediately.

Since my release from the hospital, I had become very lonely and secluded. I missed the friends I had made in those five weeks and was desperate to have someone to express my feelings with besides my family.

In June, I had gotten my wish. My mom took me down to the pet store to look at the guinea pigs. This was one of the most exciting days of my life. As we walked over to the small animal section, I saw a cage of about eight guinea pigs. Within five seconds, I knew which one to pick. There was something special about his eyes that immediately won me over. He became the only friend that I had. He was the best thing that had ever happened to me, and his name was Gilbert.

2004

In November of 2004, I was enrolled at Overlake Specialty School (O.S.S.) in Bellevue, Washington. My first day there was extremely tough. When I first glimpsed into one of the classrooms, I was reminded of everything that had gone wrong in schools previously. It was also the first time that I was within five hundred feet of another kid in a year and a half. However, the staff there was unbelievably helpful in making me feel comfortable. Their main goal for me that day, as well as in the future, was to take baby steps. I will never forget how relieved I felt when I heard that phrase. I was so accustomed to being pushed right into the middle of things and to dive headfirst into any problems I had. That is not how you handle autism, and Overlake knew that.

During that first day, I made an enormous gain. With the help of my teacher, I was able to walk into the classroom and sit down at my desk. I had my own space in the back corner of the room and was right next to the door. This was huge. Compared to all the other school experiences I had, this was paradise. My comfort level was greatly enhanced with the fact that I had an exit right next to my desk. For the first time in three years, I did not feel trapped in a classroom. Nevertheless, my anxiety was still through the roof.

For the first two weeks at O.S.S., I only attended class for half a day. When I got home, I was physically and mentally exhausted. I had made minimal contact with my classmates, usually just one or two-word responses.

Throughout my whole life, I had had a speech impediment. I could not pronounce my Ss correctly, and people had a very difficult time understanding me. This greatly enhanced my anxiety about talking to people. After I had been at Overlake for two weeks, I started attending class full-time every other day.

One of the main objectives of this school was to help kids achieve their goals. So every day, they would have us think of a goal to work on and then share it with the class. I was able to work up to reading my goals out loud. Since I had a speech impediment, I took my time thinking of how to read my goal without having to pronounce any Ss. My success rate was about 50 percent. I was somewhat confident when I did succeed, but when I didn't, I was extremely anxious and embarrassed. Despite this, all the kids took an extreme liking to me. Whenever they could, they would come up to my secluded desk to say hi and ask me questions about myself. Most of the kids at O.S.S. were there for anger issues, so they didn't have any trouble conversing. My heart would race like crazy whenever someone came up to me, but I know for a fact that if these kids did not show any interest or talk to me at all, I would never have made the strides I did at that school.

After I had been at Overlake for about three weeks, I hit a roadblock. There was this girl in my class that I knew had always liked me, but she took it too far too fast, at least for me. I opened my locker one morning and saw that she had left a note, asking me to go on a date with her. This overwhelmed me to the extreme. I didn't know what to do because I had never been in that situation before. When I walked into the classroom, she asked if I had read the note. With an annoyed look on my face, I said yes. I was making so much progress that I didn't need this kind of setback, which it was. When I got home that day, I immediately sat down on the stairs and started crying. My mom asked me what was wrong, and hesitantly, I told her. I was embarrassed to talk about it. I told her how I felt and that I needed a break from everything. She called the school and told them that I needed a day to just relax. They gladly welcomed that, so the next day, I stayed home and tried not to think about anything to do with school.

When I returned to school, the girl asked me again if I had made a decision. I told her that I hadn't. The next week or two was somewhat awkward because she kept approaching me, and I never gave her a definite answer. As the days went on, however, we became good friends, but nothing more.

2006

In the early summer of 2006, I had made so much progress that Overlake suggested I make an attempt to gradually integrate into a mainstream school in September. My family and I felt like I was capable of doing this. Plus, I decided that I wanted to play basketball for my local high school. I had always been in love with basketball, so much that I would spend two to four hours every day playing by myself. It was a great way for me to escape and to just clear my head of any unwanted thoughts that came along with having OCD. I knew that I was good enough to make it to varsity and had envisioned nothing less. So my family, along with the help of O.S.S., set up a meeting with my local high school's staff and explained to them my conditions and how we wanted to approach this transition. We decided that I would spend the first half of the day at Overlake and then spend the second half at my high school. We also met with the school's head basketball coach, Wayne Rumbaugh. We told him that I have autism and that playing basketball was one of my main goals. He seemed pretty open-minded about this and told us how the basketball program works; for example, the tryouts, summer practice, game schedules, etc. He also seemed to understand the fact that playing organized basketball would be extremely beneficial to me. After the two meetings with the school staff and basketball coach, I felt very optimistic leaving the school that morning.

Throughout the summer of 2006, the school held basketball scrimmages that were open to all students two nights a week. I made sure that I never missed a single scrimmage. I had, after all, been looking forward to this moment for over a decade. The first time I attended a scrimmage, I was very nervous. I didn't know any of the kids, and it was a totally different environment than what I was used to. The coach was there, and he introduced me to some of the players, who all seemed pretty nice. I started to relax and feel comfortable once I started shooting the ball and moving around. Exercise has always been an extremely important factor in helping me communicate with others. I was able to stay there and play for about an hour and a half. After the scrimmage was over, I was really excited and upbeat because I felt that I had accomplished something pretty impressive. I could not wait to go back again. After all my previous experiences with public schools, I never thought I'd be excited to walk back into a school. As the scrimmages progressed, I felt more and more comfortable every time. Some of the kids had taken a real liking to me even though I barely spoke.

Later that summer, however, things would take a turn for the worse. All together, there were about eight scrimmages that were on the schedule the coach gave me. Four of these scrimmages had been canceled, and not once did the coach inform us of this. It was about a twenty-five minute drive to get to the school, only to arrive and see that only the coach was there. Every time that we would ask him where everybody was, he would nonchalantly say, "Oh yeah, the scrimmage was canceled. I thought you knew." He acted like he didn't want anything to do with us, and he never even bothered to apologize. Due to my OCD, it would take me an hour just to get ready to leave for the scrimmage because I had to do everything perfectly and meticulously. The coach had wasted two hours of my day, as well as taking away the one thing that I was looking forward to that day. Taking all this into consideration, it is easy to see why I would become so angry and depressed that I would break down and cry on the way home.

It was September; summer had come and gone, and it was time for me to start taking two classes at my high school. I would spend the first half of the day at Overlake and then be taken to the high school for the second half. I was in tenth grade and was very optimistic about my attempt to attend a mainstream school. I had an individualized education plan (IEP) set up and was confident in my teachers and counselors to provide me with any support I might need. However, they failed to do that on the very first day. When I got to the school, the hallways were crammed with kids, which was extremely overwhelming for me. As fast as I could, I made my way over to my first class, which was English. Anxious to get into the classroom, where it would be much quieter, I reached for the door, but it was locked. I ended up waiting in the noisy hallway for fifteen minutes, which seemed like eternity. When the door was finally unlocked, I immediately bolted for a desk in the back. As the kids began to file in, I became more and more uncomfortable. The optimism I had experienced before had completely vanished. I was trying to get through the class as discreetly as possible when the teacher started to call each student out and to have them introduce themselves. We had had a meeting with this teacher recently and informed her that I have autism, which comes with extreme social anxiety. I was expecting her to skip me because I thought that she had actually understood my disability. Nevertheless, the time came when she asked me to stand up and introduce myself. I was mortified. I quickly shared my name, a hobby of mine, and an interesting fact about myself. I was proud of myself for having the courage to introduce myself on the spot like that, but I was also irate about what the teacher had just done to me.

My parents ended up calling her to clarify that she knew I had autism. She did indeed know but didn't quite understand why I needed special accommodations. She ended up asking my parents to write a report, her words, about the symptoms of autism and why I needed her support. My parents, as well as I, were very insulted. We had already had a meeting with her in which she told us that she understood my needs and was eager to help. Apparently, however, she forgot all about that because she did the exact opposite of what she had agreed to.

Thus far, my transition into a mainstream high school was going horribly. Nonetheless, I made a commitment to myself that I would stick it out. I am not the type to quit, especially in the face of adversity. The second class I attended was History, which was taught by the basketball coach. The first day went pretty well for there were no unexpected incidences like the class before. As the class progressed, however, things started to get out of hand. There was one day when I was on my way to history class, but when I got to the classroom, it was empty. Once again, the coach had forgotten to inform me about a change in the schedule. One of the biggest ways I stay on top of my autism is to always have a schedule, whether it is a school day or the weekend. I had no idea of what to do. I eventually headed over to my counselor's office, where he told me that the class was in the computer lab. There was no way I could attend that class because one of my biggest phobias is change, especially unexpected change. My heart was beating furiously. I told him that I was not fit to go to class and ended up reading for an hour and a half in the counselor's 10 × 10 foot office.

When I got home, I broke down and told my parents what had happened. I explained how painful and stressful the whole experience had been. They noticed that over the past week or two, I was becoming increasingly depressed. What a difference this was from earlier in the year, when I was very content with my life. We decided that public school was just not the way to go. We convened a meeting with Overlake, told them about all the things that had gone terribly awry, and decided to reinstate me there full-time. A huge weight was lifted off my shoulders. I cannot explain to you the freedom that I felt—the freedom from trying to live a normal life, the freedom from not having to be someone I'm not.

In November, the varsity basketball tryouts were to be held over a two-night period. The days leading up to the tryouts were very stressful for me while, at the same time, very exciting. The day before, I could barely hold myself together. I got in a huge argument with my sister and secluded myself for most of the day. When the tryouts finally came, I was extremely nervous as my dad was driving me to the school.

I had been waiting my whole life for an opportunity like this and was ready to prove myself.

As I walked up to the gym, I was overwhelmed to see how many kids were there. At first I was hesitant to go in, but I was not going to let my anxiety take this chance away from me. As I walked in, I saw that the coaches were lining up all the kids. I walked up to the head coach and asked him what to do. He told me to just pick a line to stand in. When I was standing in line, I noticed that all the kids were holding a blue card. Right away, I knew something was amiss. The coach started calling out names for roll call. I waited and waited and waited, but he never called my name. As I look back on it, I can't help but think how ironic this was. The one time that I wanted to have my name called out in front of a crowd of people, it didn't happen. After the roll call was over, the kids started to disperse into different groups. Once again, I walked up to the coach and asked him why my name hadn't been called. Without even looking me in the eye, he told me that I needed to be registered in able to try out and asked me for my registration card. I was dumbfounded. He had known me for more than five months and never once bothered to tell me that I needed to register in order to try out. I told him that I didn't have a card, and very bluntly he said, "You won't be able to try out tonight." I was furious. I was cheated by not having as much time to prove myself as all the other kids because, once again, the coach didn't care to communicate with me. He told me where to register and to come back tomorrow for the last night of the tryouts. As I walked out of the gym, my dad asked me what I was doing. I updated him about everything that had happened. He was in disbelief. He walked with me over to register for the next night, and then he drove me home. I felt like yelling at the top of my lungs, but as usual, I withdrew myself and resorted to crying.

The next night, as I was going through my usual routine to get ready to leave, I didn't really have any feelings toward trying out. My mom and dad drove me to the school, and I walked directly into the gym. I was put into a group with about nine other kids, and the coaches started putting us through some drills. Now as I said, I had never played organized basketball before, and the coach knew this. Nevertheless, he started calling out different plays that everyone knew but me. I had no idea of what to do and felt like an idiot wandering around the court like a lost dog. The coach got really angry with me and told me to get off the court. Who did he replace me with? His son. He vehemently praised him left and right, telling everybody that they could learn something from him. I was disgusted. I had experienced a lot of prejudice throughout my life, but this was a new low.

When the tryouts finally ended, the coaches had all the players gather around them. They handed out envelopes to each kid, which told them if they had made it to one of the three teams (varsity, junior varsity, and the C team). Not surprisingly, I was cut. I did not make it to any of the teams.

I couldn't grasp the fact that this was not a dream. It was, by far, the most devastating night of my life. I walked out of the gymnasium, went over to my parents, and broke down like never before. I thought that my life was over. I just could not fathom what had happened that night. After my parents drove me home, I was repulsed just thinking about basketball. For the next three years, I had no interest in the game.

2007

In October of 2007, my family and I moved from Auburn, Washington, to Reno, Nevada. We all needed a change in weather while also breaking free from all the bad experiences that had occurred in Washington. I still had no friends, so it was an easy decision for my family and me to make. Moving to Reno is one of the best things that have ever happened to me. My depression improved significantly just from all the sunny weather. I felt like I had a brand-new life to start.

At this point, I was still not interested in playing organized basketball. Knowing that sports are a huge outlet for me, however, I turned my attention to football. I started working out furiously and studying the game for hours a day. I was going to make sure that football would not be reminiscent of my basketball tryouts.

2008

In April of 2008, my mom and I had an IEP meeting with the staff at my local high school. The head coach of the football team was also scheduled to drop in and meet with us. As my first encounter with a high school coach was atrocious, I came into the meeting with no faith in the coach. During the meeting, he was informed that I had autism and that my goal was to play varsity football. He mentioned that he had coached a player with Asperger's syndrome at his previous school. I didn't think much of this, for our first meeting with my basketball coach had also gone well. At any rate, during this meeting, I was enrolled in a weight lifting class that was led by the coach. He was told that I had not attended a class in a public school for close to five years and that this was going to be a huge stepping stone for me. My mom and I left the meeting feeling optimistic, but that feeling didn't really mean much to me anymore.

About a week later, the day had come to attend my weight lifting class. I was extremely anxious about it, but I knew that being in a physically active class would be much easier once I became involved in it. As my mom drove me to my class, I started to have a minor panic attack. I told myself that I had to persevere through this if I was committed to playing football. My mom walked into the class with me and stayed for about ten minutes while I calmed myself down and got used to my surroundings.

Now that I was in high school, having my mom in a class with me should have been somewhat embarrassing. The kids thought nothing of it though. It was a total 180 degrees of what had happened in Washington. The coach talked with my mom for a few minutes and told her how the class works and that he'd do his best to be as helpful as possible. Again, I thought nothing of this due to my past experiences. I'm happy to say, however, that I couldn't have been more wrong.

The next two years were some of the best in my life. Both years, I was able to play varsity football, working hard enough to earn a starting spot my second year. There were times when I would have major panic attacks right before practice. As my mom would drive me to the school, I would break down and start crying. I begged her to take me home. Thankfully, she refused to. She went to tell the coach what was happening, and even though he was busy setting practice up, he came over to help me out of the car. I was in tears and very embarrassed to have him see me like that. He reminded me of what my goals were and flat out said that if I couldn't go to practice, I couldn't play football. With this is mind, I prevailed each and every time that I had a panic attack before practice.

In December, a few days after Christmas, I lost my best friend, Gilbert. When I woke up on Christmas morning, I ran over to his cage to give him his favorite breakfast, carrots. He would always come out of his wooden house, squeaking uncontrollably for food. This particular morning, however, he didn't come out. I left the carrots in his cage, thinking that he was just sleeping in. A few hours later, I walked over to his cage to give him his Christmas present, fruit-flavored cookies. Again, he did not come out of his house. I thought that he was still sleeping in. The rest of the day went by without him coming out. The day after Christmas, he came out about three times, looking really exhausted. Two days after Christmas, he was acting the same way. I finally took him out of his cage to see what the matter was. Except for looking exhausted, he seemed to be fine. So we asked our neighbor, who was a guinea pig expert, to come over and take a look. I had my mom show her Gilbert because I was too scared to hear what our neighbor might have to say. I distracted myself by watching a football game, but I couldn't help but think of the worst.

A couple minutes later, my mom came over to me and told me that he had a tumor and that he only had a few hours. I jumped up out of my chair and ran to my bedroom, trying to escape reality. I started to sob uncontrollably. My mom asked me if I wanted to see him, but I refused. I couldn't stand to see him that way. Finally, however, I agreed to hold him on my lap. For the next two hours, tears were pouring down my cheeks as Gilbert squirmed, twisted, and squeaked in pain. I stared at his precious eyes as he slowly let go. He was finally gone. I was happy for him because it was torture watching him suffer in so much pain. I stayed with him for the rest of the day, stroking him on his head and never leaving his side.

For the entire month of January, I was incapacitated with grief. I had just lost my best and only friend, and I did not know how I would survive. To this very day, I break down in tears whenever I think of him.

I had loved him with all my heart, and he loved me back.

My Best Friend

I'm back after six months
That stone had gotten to me more than once
But now it's gone
Two days back was the whisper of "so long"

It was supposed to be temporary
But it's almost been two years
I dared not to go near it just because of the fear
I was sick of wiping my face with my shirt to get the tears
But as I write this, the tears start to appear

INSIDE OUT

The pain hurts so much, and it will never go away
It's here to stay, but that's okay because it is the only way
To remember the life that we had together, and to this day
I beat myself with every single hit that I can take

I lashed out at you when all you wanted was to play
It was your way of telling me that you only had a few days
Because after that all you did was try to get away
You hid from me, but I brushed it off, a mistake that turned so
grave

I was so stupid to take for granted the life you gave to me
And when I finally asked you what was wrong, it was just too late
This wasn't fate; it was God's way to turn my life into misery

I love you so much I cannot even begin to say
All the things that I would do to spend time with you today
You were my best friend, but like I said, God took that away

I try not to think of you; No, I love you too much
When I do, my heart gets crushed, the pain, it's just too much
I guess it's self-centered, it's my emotional crutch
But this is what I signed up for, the second that we touched

I'll never forget you, Gilbert, for you turned me into a man
I was and always will be your biggest fan
People don't understand how you could be my best friend
My only friend, and in the end, I wished it was pretend

I'll never forget you, Gilbert, and you are in my heart until the end
And the end will just begin, when I see you once again

2009

In July of 2009, my football team was scheduled to attend a high school football camp for three days. The camp was in Gold Beach, Oregon, over 450 miles away. I was really excited about the camp, but as the date came closer and closer, I started to feel less excited and much more anxious. I had never spent one night away from home, except for being in the hospital. My coach had called me the best defensive end in northern Nevada, and I knew I couldn't let my teammates down. When the time had come to leave, I hesitantly walked onto the school bus. The ride was excruciating. There were two kids to a seat, and it took over twelve hours to get to the camp.

When we finally arrived, we set up our mattresses and belongings inside the local high school. There were at least eight other schools that were there. This was very overwhelming for me, for each player only had about five square feet of personal space. The very first night was very difficult for me. I had become very anxious, and I didn't know anyone enough to make me feel comfortable. I was finally able to calm myself down and go to sleep. The next morning, however, I had a panic attack. I kept it all bottled inside because I didn't want anyone to know that I was scared of being away from home. I called my mom and gave her an update about what was going on. I told her that I really wanted to come home and that I didn't think that I could handle three more days of this. She told me to use my coping skills and to just relax for the moment. About five minutes after we ended our call, my coach waved me over from across the room. I stood up from my bed and walked over to him. He told me that my mom had called to let him know what my condition was. We took a walk out of the school and over to his RV, where we sat down and talked for a good forty-five minutes. There was a beautiful view of the ocean in front of us, and the smell of the saltwater really helped calm me down. We talked about all the great things that I had accomplished since joining the football team and how I found the courage to accomplish this feat. He gave me the option of going home early if I didn't think I could handle it. Even though I really wanted to go home, I was very opposed to the idea. I did not want to let anyone down, especially my coach and the team itself. For the next three days, I was able to block all the negative thoughts and worries in my head and ended up having some of the best days of my life. The only thing that I could not stop dreading was the torturous twelve-hour bus ride home.

At the end of the 2009 football season, I had made tremendous progress with my social anxiety and communication skills. Over the last two years, which were some of the best in my life, I had really enjoyed the camaraderie of my teammates. I was not able to play at the level everyone expected me to that year because I had lost all the cartilage in my big right toe. Every time that I took a step, bone was rubbing on bone, and it was excruciatingly painful. However, there was no way I was going to sit out the season, so I gritted my teeth and was able to play in every game. I finished tied for the team lead in sacks and lead all defensive ends in tackles. I had surgery two months after the season.

At the end of the season banquet in November, our coach brought each player up, one by one, and gave a short thirty-second speech about them. I was waiting and waiting for my name to be called, but it turned out that I was the last one chosen. I walked over to the coach, and he gave an unbelievable six-minute speech about all the obstacles that I had overcome and how proud he was of me. This was definitely one of the proudest moments of my life. Near the end of the speech, my coach started to tear up, describing me as a role model for all the kids out there with autism. A couple tears started to fall from my own eyes. It meant so much to me that he gave that speech. Nobody had ever done something like that before. To top it off, a few moments later, I was named to the Nevada All-State Academic Team. I will definitely never forget that night.

2011

When 2011 came around, I was really excited about playing college football. I would have to move out of my parents' house in June and live by myself two hundred miles away. I thought that I was ready to take on this challenge, but when June came closer and closer, my family and I began to realize how unrealistic the situation was. We had a lengthy discussion about the move, and I had come to terms that there was no way I was going to be able to live by myself two hundred miles away without knowing anyone around, all while having to attend school, which I was deathly afraid of. Even though it broke my heart and crushed my dream, I ended up deciding not to play college football. It turned out that I wouldn't be able to play anyway because my big toe that I had surgery on was becoming increasingly painful. If I were to play, I would risk severely injuring it, with the risk of having to have the joints fused together.

In March of 2011, I was set to go on my very first date. I was extremely excited because I didn't have anyone to talk to or hang out with besides my family. I had psyched myself up the whole week before the date and was ready to give it my best shot. It was one of the happiest weeks of my life. The morning of the date, however, I received a text from her saying that she had been hit with an ear infection and would not be able to make it. I replied by saying that I hope she recovers soon and to let me know when she wants to reschedule. After a few days, I had not heard from her, so I sent her another text, asking how she felt. I never heard from her again. I was crushed. I went into a deep depression for about a week. Once again, I had thought that something was finally going to go my way for a change. I was naive to think that.

I'm a Fool for You

I've already fallen for you, but I don't even know you
We haven't even met, but somehow I adore you
I can't get you out of my head; thoughts of you are stuck like glue
The pain is starting to progress; I am depressed without you

We're supposed to meet each other, but something's telling me we won't
I've got to get this mess together; I'm going insane being alone
I'm waiting in the rain for you; I guess that I'll go home
The flowers drop to the ground, as I trace back this lonely road

I need to be with you, I'll wait for you, just to be cruel
A broken heart will be my death; I'll put away the rope and stool
I'll throw my whole life away, if it means that we'll be two
I'm a fool, but I don't care, this is all that I can do

I ended up going on my first date in June with a girl named Danielle. I was very nervous. Once we saw each other, however, it was amazing how much I opened up and talked. I had never talked that much to a stranger in my whole life. The date ended up going great, and we met again a few days later to have lunch in the park. I talked even more this time. It was amazing how comfortable I felt around her. It was another great date, and we decided to hang out again later that week. Two days later, I called her and asked what she wanted to do. She hesitantly told me that she didn't think we should see each other again. When I asked her why, she responded by telling me that I reminded her too much of her ex-boyfriend and that she had met someone else.

Once again, my heart was ripped out and stepped on. She was my only friend, and I did not want to lose her. We stopped communicating with each other once she told me her decision was final. I was baffled. How is it that whenever something is going right for me, it turns out that it was all just a joke? I ended up going into another deep depression, staying in my room for hours, thinking about her and crying nonstop. I hated my life. I always had faith that my life would someday get easier. Whenever that seemed to happen, however, it took a turn for the worse.

On July 1, I moved out of my parents' house and into my own apartment. This was an enormous step for me. I was excited to become much more independent and to have a place I could call my own. It was my very first night in my apartment when I received a text from Danielle. It had been over two weeks since we stopped talking, and I had finally started to get over her. She asked me how I liked my apartment and told me she was happy for me. After texting for a while, I ended up asking her if she wanted to come over and check it out sometime. She excitedly said yes, and she came over two days later. The night she came over, we ended up talking for four hours. That was, by far, the longest I had ever talked to anyone my whole life. She told me that things weren't working out with the other guy, and so we made plans to see each other again in a couple of days. After about three more dates, I asked her if she wanted to be together. With a big smile, she said yes and told me how special I was to her. This was one of the happiest moments in my life. It was so surreal I could not believe it. We started to hang out more often, every date being better than the last. Before I moved, I was worried about being depressed and lonely in my apartment. Having a girlfriend, though, was all I needed to live a happy life.

The next month was the best in my life. Things had indeed worked out for me, and I thanked God every night for that. One day, I texted Danielle and asked her if she wanted to go out to dinner one night. She told me that she couldn't because she already had plans. She also told me that she had decided to go back to her abusive ex-boyfriend. She didn't think we should see each other again. My heart stopped. I was in complete shock. She had told me repeatedly that she was never getting back together with her ex, and yet she did. This blow did me in. I felt like my life was over. I have never been suicidal and never will be, but that day was the closest I had ever come to getting there. Even though I would never pull the trigger on myself, I was craving for a gun. I was, however, thinking of seriously hurting her ex. He was extremely abusive to her and controlled every aspect of her life. If I ended up getting arrested for doing something extreme, I would have been glad to embrace jail or even prison. At least then I would have structure in my day and be around other people, instead of sitting alone all day in my apartment. I was so devastated that I cannot begin to describe my feelings. I did, however, try to in a letter I wrote to Danielle.

Dear Danielle,

I do not want this letter to cause you any guilt, but I need you to know the pain I am feeling. I am not lying when I say you are one of the best things that have ever happened to me. Yes, we have only known each other for 6 weeks, but I know a special person when I see one. I don't know if I have told you this, but 8 years ago I was admitted to Children's Hospital in Seattle to help treat my OCD, depression and anxiety. I was in there for 5 weeks of pure hell. I would have much preferred being in jail for those weeks. At least then I wouldn't have any mental disabilities destroying my life.

The last time I had a friend was in 2001. The past 10 years have been excruciatingly lonely and depressing, along with feelings that would take years of explaining for someone to understand. Hundreds of times I have cried myself to sleep at night, hoping and praying that I would soon find a friend.

When we met for the first time on June 11, it was my first experience hanging out with someone besides my family in over a decade. I was extraordinarily nervous before I actually saw you. But when I did see you, there was something about you that made me open up and talk like no one else has made me before. I know that you thought that I was really shy that night, but I totally exceeded my expectations of how much I thought I'd talk that night. I was on cloud 9 that night, as well as every other time we have hung out. We had only met once, but it was such a huge step for me in my life that I was starting to think would never come.

When you texted me a couple of days after our second date, explaining that you had found someone else that you connected with more, I was in so much pain that it was indescribable. I know that you did nothing wrong and that you had every right to choose to stop seeing me. After 2 ½ weeks, I was just starting to get over you. Yes I added you on Facebook, but the very first night at my new place you texted me for the first time in 2 weeks. It led to me asking if you ever wanted to come over and check my place out. You said yes, and that night we ended up talking for 3 ½ hours, the longest I had ever talked to someone. About a week later I asked if you wanted to be together and you said yes. That was one of the happiest moments of my life. You had told me multiple times how bad your ex treats you and that you were not going to get back together with him. If I had known that you still had feelings for him, I would have never asked you to be committed with me.

You also told me that he was being very nice all of a sudden just because he was jealous of you seeing someone else. I expressed to you my fear of losing you, and was reassured when you told me that we would eventually end up being together and that everything About 12 days ago, you told me that you were not ready to be in a relationship and that you needed to take some time to just clear your head of everything. You told me how your ex kept contacting you saying that he wanted to get back together, and flipped out every time would work out between us. I was more than willing to give you the space and time that you needed to get things straight. On July 22, we went to the marina to just hang out and chat. You brought up the topic of our relationship and asked me how I felt about it. You even asked me if I was worried that you and your ex would get back together. I told you that I knew you two would not get back together, but that my fear of that was always in the back of my mind. I hope that at this time you had not already made up your mind about your ex and you, because if you had, I really wish you would have told me then and there. I was still very excited about meeting your family, and was really looking forward to taking you out to dinner.

On Monday I asked if you wanted to hang out on Tuesday. All of a sudden, however, and out of the blue, you told me that you were seeing your ex again. You told me that deep down, you really want it to work with him, even though you're sure it won't. I was devastated and I still am. You broke my heart Danielle.

I don't want you to think that I am writing this letter out of spite and that I want you to feel guilty. I just really want to tell you the absolute truth about how I feel. You have been the reason I have done so well living by myself. You often ask if I get lonely. I do, but texting with you every day and looking forward to hanging out with you was all that I needed. Like I said before, you are the only true friend I have and have had. I cannot express the feelings I have about you entering my life.

I am not trying to win the sympathy vote in hopes that you will come back. I want you to follow your heart. I just want to let you know that I will wait in case things don't work out, but obviously it is your choice if you ever want to see me again or hang out. I'll always have my phone with me in case you ever want to talk.

Sincerely,
Russell

I spent a very long time composing that letter and trying to capture all my feelings in it. My keyboard was soaked with tears once I had finished. I was not myself after this whole ordeal. I mentally broke down multiple times a day. No one could understand the pain I was feeling. I lost my only friend I had had in over ten years and knew I would never see her again. She might have just as well died.

I ended up entering a deep depression, which lasted for months. I couldn't bear living in my apartment by myself, so in August I moved back in with my parents. I would stay at my place for a couple of hours every so often, but that was it.

Untitled

Monday was the day that you paralyzed me with pain
Destroying my whole world with the most unbearable strain
Of depression that I maintained for weeks without any gains
All the while leaving a stain on my heart that you ripped and maimed

That day was the closest that I had ever maintained
The thought of having my brains rain
Upon my lifeless body from a colt .45 aimed
At the origin of all things gained, at the origin of all my pain

You tore me up, but now I'm coming back stronger
Yes, I'm still depressed, but yet I am no longer
Unsure of my will to live on, an idea so heavily pondered
Those thoughts are collected and are now much calmer

I sang a song so somber
But the harp's strings are being pulled no longer
What you did was neither right nor wrong
You killed the feelings I had forever longed for

They say that everything happens for a reason
Hinting that everything will soon work itself out
But what if that everything goes back on its promise?
Like my everything did, burying my heart six feet down

I dream of seeing you again, but I know that dream will not come true
I'm moving on without you, for I now know I'm too good for you
You made me want to kill from all the sadness that you brewed
But the only thing I will kill are the memories of being with you

For the last couple of years, I have obsessed about my body image. Recently, it has gotten so bad that I was diagnosed with anorexia and body dysmorphic disorder (BDD). I have to work out extremely hard every day, or else I worry excessively about what I eat. Even though I have 6 percent body fat (the average male body fat is 15-22 percent), I am very hesitant to take off my shirt when going to the beach or swimming in a pool. I work out so much that when I do take a day off, my metabolism is extremely high and I'm usually very hungry. Around the end of July, I started to starve myself on the days I did not work out. I was losing a lot of weight (6 lbs. in ten days), and my family was worried about me. They could definitely tell that I was losing a lot of my muscle mass. I was so afraid of gaining the littlest amount of fat that the feeling of being hungry was much better than feeling the mental pain of my OCD. I know that I can eat anything I want and still have the same physique, but the pain of obsession was just too much to handle. I have not eaten a single desert, candy, or any other so-called junk food in over two years. I always eat a big dinner, and even when I have worked out and lifted weights for over two hours, I can feel fat building and drooping down instantaneously on my chest. I know that there is no way possible for that to happen, but my OCD overrides any sanity that I have left that day.

Lately, my OCD has focused specifically on saturated fats. I have cut out about half of what I used to eat a few months ago. I love pizza, but it hurts my brain too much to even have one slice. My favorite dinner is spaghetti and sausage, but now I just have plain spaghetti while my family eats the regular meal. I won't eat cheese of any kind, ground beef, turkey and yogurt (unless they are fat-free), nuts, protein bars, the list goes on and on. Every single food that I have cut out of my diet is one of my favorite foods to eat. I used to eat them with no problem. I would be able to happily enjoy five to seven slices of pizza, and I didn't gain one bit of fat. Right now, I am too obsessed about my body that I can't even comprehend eating those foods. I will try not to eat more than 5 grams of saturated fat before dinner. To put that into perspective, a man who burns approximately 3,800–4,300 calories a day, as I do, consumes an average of 45-60 grams of saturated fat per day.

On an average day, I will lift my shirt up and look in the mirror about ten to fifteen times. After I eat, I can see places with fat that weren't there before I ate. I know my brain is playing visual tricks with me, but it is amazing how real it looks.

On September 23, 2011, I had surgery on my right big toe for the second time. A few months back, I started receiving the same excruciating amount of pain that I did in 2009. My doctor gave me a Kevlar insert to wear in my shoe so that my toe would not bend when walking or running. This immediately relieved me of any pain that I had. However, once again things just didn't go my way. It turned out that before I had received my implant, I had subconsciously altered the way I walked, due to the pain I was feeling. This eventually ended up fracturing my left foot. I wore a walking boot for six weeks and even used a state-of-the-art ultrasound bone healing system. When the time came to take the boot off, I was extremely excited. However, when the doctor took an x-ray of my foot to make sure that the bone had healed, it turned out that it did not heal at all. I cannot describe how frustrated I was. Adding to that, my toe started to hurt again, which lead to my second surgery. The cause of the pain was large amounts of bone spurs growing underneath the previous incision mark. Instead of continuing to wear the boot and be inactive, I decided to wait until after the surgery to wear it, attempting to kill two birds with one stone. As of right now, I am currently wearing two boots, praying that everything heals successfully this time.

This autobiography was very difficult for me to write. Having dealt with all the problems and disorders in my life has made me extremely confident, amazingly dedicated to anything I set my mind on, and very understanding. This book is intended to spread the word about autism and to let others know what it is like living with it. It is also intended to help people understand more about high-functioning autism, especially in adults.

"Never, never, never quit."

-Winston Churchill

The Hurricane

As I look through the window of the tower lit high
The spread of the ocean forever moves
Everywhere, the rocks protrude

The mystic sky, dark with fury
Reflects its visage against the waves
The sight of an augury

The atmosphere around, so sordid indeed
The rage is so pertinent
Cloud nine is absent

The wickedness of its eye
It shall be malignant
The horror it shall imply

I stand witness to this view
My eyes soon succumb
My thoughts become numb

The curse draws closer
How dismal and odious
For there is no answer

The sea grows dark
The tower's light is no more
The demon has come ashore

The victims so negligible
For their unknown fate
Will never be livable

The doom has arrived
There is no transition
As all collide

Everything so decrepit
All is to rot
The horror has been brought

Wars Will Never End

The wars have started long ago
For wars will never end
The women and children, all in woe
As their souls gradually ascend

The deep depression that strikes one's mind
Dreadfully stays its course
For in time, one's thoughts grow blind
And soon show signs of no remorse

The darkness that prevails the light
Is guided by its master
The orders given are in spite
For ignorance leads to disaster

The bliss was taken long ago
The misery will never end
The women and children will someday know
That their souls have reached their end

The Conscience of Man

Little do we know
That inside of us
grow Miniature men
Who fight for our souls

Some good, some bad
Some sad, some glad
To most seem transparent
When one's out to gad

They look after our species
Though they rarely agree
On the decisions we make
For our blind eyes they foresee

The trouble we make
In the events we partake
Are none for their pleasure
They recognize our mistake

But who shall guide them?
In their troubles that stem
From the ignorant thoughts
Of their shell that is man

For they venture alone
In the dark they condone
They shall fight no more
Their weakness has shown

INSIDE OUT

Free from their shell
They no longer dwell
In their shell's hollow heart
For their ship has set sail

A soul unprotected
A soul now infected
With nerves of pure ice
Is a soul now neglected

The love is no more
The heart is ignored
The mind is a follower
To its master no more

So soon said and done
The evil has won
For in hell awaits
The end of their run

Hail to the Earth!

Hail to the Earth, for she may never perish!
Hail to the Earth, for all life she will reminisce!
Hail to the Earth, for all the minds she has brought forth!
Hail to the Earth, for to all life she gave birth!

Hail to the pastures, all plastered with green!
Hail to the seas, for they are the kings!
Hail to the gods, who protect all our sights!
Hail to the Earth, for she is our light!

Hail to the doves, whose peace we adore!
Hail to the trees, whose love is evermore!
Hail to the valleys, which offer a choice!
Hail to the Earth, for she is our voice!

Hail to the mountains, which proffer hope when one's in doubt!
Hail to the clouds, which prevail through our droughts!
Hail to the streams, for they restore our hearts!
Hail to the Earth, for she was our start!

Hail to the life, which encircles our minds!
Hail to the times, for our paths they define!
Hail to the words, which advance our race!
Hail to the Earth, for she is our saving grace!

Hail to the feelings, which direct our scruples!
Hail to the friendship, which fills all our holes!
Hail to the failures, for they guide our directions!
Hail to the Earth, for she is our protection!

Hail to the love, for without it our souls would fade!
Hail to the misery, for its absence shall void pray!
Hail to the hate, for there would be no good!
Hail to the Earth, for all she has withstood!

Hail to the Earth, for she may never perish!
Hail to the Earth, for all life she will reminisce!
Hail to the Earth, for all the minds she has brought forth!
Hail to the Earth, for to all life she gave birth!

A Day in Darfur

His name was Jabari from the city of the slain
There was no one in sight as his body lay maimed
For hours and hours at this spot he laid
His feelings were numb as he continued to pray
His world was now empty with nothing in sight
His body left behind as his soul saw the light

His brothers, his sisters
They all face these crimes
His brothers, his sisters
They know nothing of these crimes

The yard will be full, it has been full
The red crosses have been struck
Their bodies are salvaged by silk and needle
The rest is up to luck

For years it has ensued, and for years it will not pass
The flames that one encounters is nothing new, alas
All rule appears inept, the dwellers weak and frail
No hope for help to come, for the anguish will prevail

Egos Will Kill

The congregates all stared at him
What a despicable-looking man!
With a face of white and an eerie grin
No being would be his friend

Each pair of eyes would stalk him
What a lift of self-esteem!
No more their lives, depressing and grim
For they have been redeemed!

A wicked sight this surely was
An oral slaying of one's heart
His soul will soon rise, and at their cost
Their lives will fall apart

Nothing

There is nothing, nothing, my thoughts are just nothing
How could I be here if everything is nothing?
For I do not know what was, I know not what will be
My eyes look around, but there is nothing to see

I stand here alone, but how do I know
If everything is nothing, how *could* I know?
Why keep myself company when there is nothing to be?
I stand here alone, for I am nothing to me

I know not what is nothing, it means nothing to me
But how do I know it means nothing to
me? All these thoughts merely mean not a
thing
If everything is nothing, then what could nothing mean?

Nothing knows me, it knows me well
How could it be that it knows me so well?
I have nothing to fear, for I now know what it means
The real meaning of nothing is the real meaning of me

Positive Opponents

The devil is strange
How strange would I say?
Strange enough to punish fiends
When we think he's depraved

Villains are good
How good would I say?
Good enough to teach us sense
When their faults are displayed

Words are too simple
How simple would I say?
Simple enough
But too complex to explain

Virtues are dire
How dire would I say?
Dire enough to let loose egos
And make one's character dissipate

Thoughts are obscure
How obscure would I say?
Obscure enough to deal out conflict
When there is no need to debate

Dark Side of Me

This is the dark side of me that no one has ever seen before
I've let it out from my heart, and now it is no more ignored
Released into the state of me that I've never before explored
I've turned my back on my soul, the very thing that I've adored
Since I was young, to which I clung, when my back was against the door
And I now have myself asking questions that I've never asked before
Who am I, where am I, is my old life now no more?
I've taken the wrong exit before, and until yesterday I still had sworn
To the lord that I will fight with all my might just to save my rapport
With myself, when things get rough, but that part of me is no more

I've shed my skin, it's in the trash, it's in the past, this time surpassed
By greater good, or so I'm told; this dark side of me will outlast
Any gracious thoughts of mine, most of which have already passed
From my mind to the dirt, six feet under the wilting grass

If I do not know you, then why should I care about you?
Don't come to me; don't talk to me, for I will look right through you
My respect for others is no more, please don't get this wrong, for this is true
The dark side of me has come out, and there is nothing you can do

My Dream

My dream is just that
It's a dream they all say
A life so luxurious
A dream so cliché

"Be realistic!" they proclaim
It's a statement of control
I disregard their ignorance
As I know what my hard work is for

They criticize me,
"That will not be your life!"
This just adds fuel
To my fire that is rife

Why should I give up?
What point would that have?
It would make my life worthless,
No purpose to be had

They should know better
Than to underestimate me
My drive will never stop
My drive they'll never beat

Troubled Young Kid

"People like you don't deserve to live!"
These were the thoughts of a troubled young kid
The quote likely aimed at people he feared
His thoughts were as real as his intentions were clear

The Key to My Heart

It's the key to my heart, the depiction that is missing
Determined when I read into it, but then the book goes missing
The nighttime is the best time, without a doubt it's true
I look forward to the morning but dread the afternoon
It's at night that I'm alive; my need is to take action
This need is blocked by me; I do not take advantage of this passion
Bottom line, every day, declines me of my mind
I might as well be sleeping, which is my better time

The Day Is Over

The day is over, yet today has just begun
My mind is killing me, what do I do? My life is done
Make it literal! Go to the closet, pick up your gun
It's loaded, cocked, and ready to have some fun

What the hell am I doing here, living a life like this?
Is your life a lie? Why the hell do you exist?
I have no love in my life, not even one damn kiss
That's why you have a gun; don't go cut your goddamned wrists!

All this is getting to me, all that is inside
That's why you have me here, so I can tell you when to die
Now go and get your gun, pull the trigger, give it a try
If you do it properly, this will be our last good-bye

I'll walk over to the closet and pick up the gun for you
That's a good boy; grip it tight, you know what to do
All I want is a better life! Will this make my dream come true?
All you need to know is that this is long overdue

Iraq Invades

Little Jimmy looks out of the front door
At what seems to be a beautiful day
This is untrue for Jimmy though
For those thoughts have gone away

His heart is racing
Sweat is dripping from his brow
He takes a deep breath and takes a step
He is so frightened to go out

He can't take any more of these sights
Blood over here, blood over there
Bodies maimed right in front of his eyes
It's no wonder he's so scared

His best friend was killed when he stepped on a mine
His big brother, sent to God's lair
How foolish he was, for he got in the line
Of fire, bullets spewing everywhere

Jimmy is oh so angry
Angry of the red, white, and black
Which, in the center, states, "God is great"
But to Jimmy, God has turned his back

On the fighting that is going on
Among his human beings
Killing one another with guns and bombs
Or at least that is how it seems

INSIDE OUT

The smell of death is haunting
As is the stench of burning skin
Every day seems never ending
This world is far too sick for him

He has seen bodies melt,
All turning to slush
Lonely limbs on the ground
And faces that have been crushed

Jimmy used to love his life; his world had seemed so grand
Until his country was attacked, or as they say protect
This war was for the greater good, man versus man
Some geniuses they had to be, it had the opposite effect

His neighborhood is no more
All the houses are torn apart
Everyone trying to escape the horror
As the red, white, and black begin to march

Jimmy cannot take this anymore
All the death and gore that he sees
Mangled bodies, tied in hordes
He wants to be set free

He finally takes that second step,
For he's not scared anymore
All the fight that he once had left
He now knows what to do, unlike before

He walks down the street toward the base
The base of the red, white, and black
And proceeds to stare the men in the face
As he reaches behind his back

This war will never be understood
In survivors' broken minds
This war will never stand for good
It has broken the red line

I'm Happy

Don't think I'm not a happy person
Don't think I don't know how to have fun
Maybe it's just that I want to blend in
Maybe I just want to be you for once

You start to talk to me and act real happy
I get sick of that, so I ignore you
You might think I'm rude, you might think I'm mean
Well, you've got it wrong, I'm just jealous of you

You don't know me; you think my life is just like yours
Oh, I'm sorry, you don't have any friends?
When you talk, your mind gets taken over by nerves?
I don't think so, so put those thoughts to an end

You're lucky your mind isn't messed up
You're lucky that you have an active life
Why is it my life that had to be snubbed?
Rejected by you with no contrite

Discrimination Kills

A black man was walking down the street, going home
A car drove by, shot him point-blank, now he's gone
He left behind a family—wife, daughter, and son

A gay was walking down the street, all covered in blood
Three bullets in his head and two punctured lungs
In five steps he collapsed, the victim of three men having fun

A Jew was walking down the street, happy as can be
Three minutes later, he was cornered into a back alley
He was jumped at, mugged, and thrown into the street

A white man was walking down the street
Eager to get home to his beautiful family
This feat he did complete, for he was left in peace

A Soon-to-Be Victim

A soon-to-be victim has come into my sights
A gun in my left hand, a knife in my right
This man in front of me destroyed my whole life
The last breath he will draw will be drawn tonight

He acted like my friend, but he doesn't know me
He acted like I'm slow, but that's contradictory
I just tuned him out, for there was no point of listening
He kept moving his lips, but I don't hear what I see

Let's not get into details; it would take me my whole day
I'll just say his act elevated each and every way
He filled me with rage, much to my dismay
And that's why I have chosen to end his life today

God Made Me Who I Am

God made me who I am today
God took me to where I am today
He helped me behave in a way
That was impossibly fitting
To be locked into my soul
And be progressive without
My brain is shouting at me
Because I won't let it out
I can't help but keep it confined
Inside of my mind that once died
At the age of twelve, but has since been revived

I probably won't let it out
In fear of being a freak
Rain gut of the top of the, gut of the rain for the top of the
That's my head's motto every time I speak
To that guy in the gym whom I never wanted to meet
Or any other person that I come across in the streets

So leave it to me
To be all that I can be
Even if that means I freeze
When you try to warm up to me

Mr. Halley

Year 1692 is when that blasphemous buffoon
Revealed the dwellings of a man's mind
A song of sorrow tune

In hollow earth his thoughts aren't welcome
I put forth fire on my everlasting
Souls that were in tombs

He shall not last in man's own head
For their psyches reside with me
And slumber in my bed

My home, he thought, is bright as day
He knew not it is the flames
Feeding on likes of him for play

The expanding air of my own singed lives
Releases to the world above
Making for the glacial lights

Dare not his ideas flow
Through the river of the blood
Ensuing to the float to those unbeknownst

Down! Down! I'll come to pluck him from the sky
Twenty-one grams smothered in a fire
So hot the blaze will cry

Soon, not enough, he will accompany me
Into my dear bed
Filled with minds—temper free

Hesitance not taken to his own wit's dying out
It is his time to be tucked in
No more spews from his shriveled spout

Invincible in future times of the past and present
I shall remain the captor of all thoughts
Mr. Halley, you will learn your lesson

*Edmond Halley was an English astronomer, geophysicist, mathematician, and
meteorologist recognized for computing the orbit of Halley's Comet, which later took his
name. In 1692, Halley proposed a theory that the Earth was hollow.*

Your Poem

You asked me to write a poem for you
Which I agreed to do
I'll just keep it short and simple
This is what I think of you

You seem like a wonderful person
Who knows how to listen
Who also understands
And never asks the wrong questions

I still have a lot to learn about you
Which I am excited to do
You still have a lot to learn about me
And I hope you're excited too

You asked me to write a poem for you
Which I agreed to do
I'll just keep it short and simple
This is what I think of you

Carve My Heart

My mind, my soul
Don't take it away
If you lose my faith today
My respect for you will stray

The crash of these waves
Will soon spray the array
Of the spite you displayed
When you paved the way

For all hell to break loose
I can still feel the blaze
Of the fire that you made
From the hatred that you gave

Your actions have played
That same somber song of faith
With the break in the middle
Of the *F* and the *H*

So bring with you your blade
For I'll give way to the pain
I'll give way to your ways
Of the vindictiveness you crave

So here I am, take what you may
Carve my heart out today

Life: It's a Game

Every day, I'd wake up to play the same damn game
I'd take my dose of pride to face the boss of this domain
Wash it down with fear; I took some strides but made no gains
All the kids ever tried to do was f— with my brain

I kept to myself; I never bothered anyone
Maybe unintentionally because of how pathetic I'd become
I was so scatterbrained; I let down my family as a son
I was so worthless, not even fit to be the victim of a gun

I would stare at the wall, zoned out, deep thoughts accompanying music
You told me I was accomplishing s—. Madam, screw it
Your behavior was so transparent; don't even try to make excuses
Your job was your life; I was your pawn and you damn well knew it

Get Well

You have no friends
You have that special wish that you commend
You finally met the person of your dreams
But f— the feeling, it's pretend

You were so excited; you were climbing the ladder of love
But then you fell down the rungs; you're starting to think that there's
 no one above
That watches over you; instead he watches you!
He torments you! Like a f—ing flat tire your heart blew

You wish you could go back, back to when you were ten
Your were so popular; yes, sir, you were the man
But that f——in' metal in your mouth didn't give a damn
Blow your f—ing brains out! In this life a chance you didn't stand

But this is now; there's no denying the last ten years have been pure
hell
Robbed of a childhood, your heart pounded while your brain swelled
Your old friends walked the bridge over the pit where you just fell
But now I guess the time has come to stop dwelling and get well

The Wild Hunt

Close your eyes, my boy, for the hounds have arrived
Descending from the sky
Gwynn app Nudd, king of Annwn[1]
Leads them on with his dreadful cry

Dare not, my boy, sleep today
Keep your spirit tightly bound
For if you partake in your dreams
In their parade you will be found

Thou shall not, my boy, take interest
In this hunt for the Moss Maiden[2]
Lest you be snatched by wicked hands
Who'll bring you to their deathly haven

Fear not, my boy, for we have no control
Of the outcome that has been destined
There is blood to be spilt or a plague to be spread
Ensuing the sure death of kith and kin
We are, my boy, fated to be prey
Of this wild hunt before us
So take part with me to relish this sight
Before we hear the devil's chorus

[1] In Welsh mythology, Gwynn app Nudd was the leader of the underworld, known as Annwn.
[2] In German folklore, the Moss people were fairies who were "grey and old-looking, hairy, and clad in moss" (Thiselton-Dyer, 1889).

Kent State

A gruesome day in 1970, blood was splattered about
The bodies of innocent ones were lying facedown
A young man was shot once, collapsing to the ground
In memoriam Jeffery, your spirit abounds

Just nineteen years old, constructing a quote of pure peace
Allison stared death straight in the eyes
Not at all afraid of what she was to meet
Her essence conquered her demise

Paranoia unfortunately set its eyes upon Bill
An innocent passerby of pure hell
A man so young, his whole life he had to fulfill
Not again would he hear the toll of the bell

A walk across the green turned into a resting in the red
For young Sandra, a woman of smarts and compassion
For a bullet was approaching her, aimed just below her head
A death brought about in such a ruthless fashion

Thirteen innocent victims, four of whom perished
Were tossed into a world of such mayhem
All lives of such value, always to be cherished
May such a calamity never happen again